Amazon Echo Dot

The complete user guide and manual for quickly mastering your Amazon Echo Dot

Logan Styles

D1563367

Table Of Contents

Conclusion

Introduction

I want to thank you and congratulate you for downloading the book *Amazon Echo Dot: The complete user guide and manual for quickly mastering your Amazon Echo Dot.*

This book contains user friendly information on how to manage your special Amazon tool. Tips for using the AI app Alexa, a step by step process in how to set up your new Dot, and a growing list of many skills the Dot can use.

Here's something that you need to be aware of: Amazon Echo Dot, and even Amazon Echo, are very hard to come by. Not only do you have to be an Amazon Prime member, but you also have to voice your order through Amazon Fire TV or the Amazon App (or even through an Amazon Echo if you already have one). And they won't come in within the first day either. You'll just be put on the wait-list.

If you already have an Amazon Echo Dot ordered and squared away, then you are set. You can read this ebook in confidence that you'll get what you want. But if you're reading this before deciding if you want to or not, then it's probably not for you. Unless you're seriously considering setting up an order through your Amazon Prime account. By all means, do it. You can still read this while you wait for it to ship in.

Without further ado, here's the extensive knowledge on how to manage your very own Echo Dot.

Chapter 1: What is the Amazon Echo Dot?

The Amazon Echo Dot is a small, black, compact speaker that can fit in the palm of your hand. The shape and size is equivalent to a hockey puck, so it is fairly small and can fit just about anywhere you want it too. Put it in a drawer, or by a book case, it saves more space than the original Amazon Echo. And just like the Amazon Echo, the Echo Dot uses voice recognition to activate its many features, including Bluetooth Speakers and Alexa. These features, which will each be explained in depth in later chapters, include seven microphones, built-in speakers, Bluetooth capabilities to connect to other speakers and/or wifi, and can answer any verbal question through Alexa.

There are no screens or other forms of interaction — aside from setting it up with Amazon's smartphone app, the Dot is designed to be fully controlled with voice commands, and has the same range of response as its older, taller sibling.

The Echo Dot is meant to be the cheaper and cost-friendly alternative to the original Amazon Echo, but more differences will be explained further in the following chapter. The Dot's own features will be explained and compared in the chapter as well.

In your ordered box (as you can only order Amazon Echo Dot through Alexa) you get the device in question, a 3.5 millimeter audio cable, a 9W power adapter, a USB charging cable, and a Quick Start Guide book.

Chapter 2: The Difference between Echo, Tap and Echo Dot

Visual Differences

The Amazon Echo, Amazon Tap, and Amazon Echo Dot are all unique Amazon Bluetooth devices; they have it in the name no less. Visually, the difference between them can be compared into size. The original Echo is the tallest, and resembles a typical speaker you see hooked up to old computer monitors. It shares many of the same features as the Echo Dot, and the Dot can even be compared to looking like the exact top section of the regular Echo.

Meanwhile, the Tap has the look and feel of a remote control. As the Tap is battery powered and can be recharged, you can take it wherever you go. However, there is a limit to where you can use it without wifi as the Tap cannot connect to you if you're out in the park. This can be remedied with mobile hot-spots via your smartphones. Any time you want to talk or ask the Tap something, you have to press the microphone button as it doesn't respond to the wake word "Alexa".

The Echo is the tallest and most powerful, as well as costing the most at $180. The Tap, sacrificing a bit of size and power for portability, rounds out at about $130. And the Echo Dot with its small stature is the cheapest at $90.

If one would put the Echo Dot near the top of the Echo, they would notice a very striking resemblance. They share the same volume ring on top that controls the internal speaker volume, the external wired volume and (in the case of the Dot only) wireless Bluetooth speakers. They have the same buttons on the same places, and the same microphones surrounding the blue glowing circle.

What you probably don't know is that the speakers on the Dot face down, and the bottom base has vent holes for the sound to escape. Since the Echo Dot sticks fast to any surface, the design choice allows for sound to bounce off the surface the Dot is on.

Hardware Differences

Again, the Tap uses a rechargeable battery, which allows for portable access on the go and to connect to other wifi-friendly sources. The Echo and Echo Dot are meant for home use, and are plugged via power adapters. They are all wifi compatible at 802.11a/b/g/n, but while the Tap uses only a single-band of 2.4 GHz processing power, the Echos both use a dual-band (2.4 GHz AND 5 GHz).

All three devices can activate through the action/microphone button, but the Tap is excluded from the use of the Wake Word, I.E. Alexa. Speaking of buttons, the Tap has four to use; the microphone/talk button, the power button, a button to enable Wifi/Bluetooth, and a button for dedicated playbacks. Both of the Echos only have action and mute buttons. All three Amazon devices have light rings along their top surfaces that glow whenever Alexa is activated. It goes without saying that they all come with the Alexa App, too.

Interestingly, despite the larger size, the Echo only carries Mono speakers. But the larger size allows the sound to carry out better than the other devices. As for the small Tap and even smaller Echo Dot, they both use Stereo speakers. The Tap is the only device to come with Dolby Audio.

The ability to receive commands, however, is not really that different between the Echo and Echo Dot. Despite the former bearing strong speakers, they are both likely to pick up your voice at the same time when issuing a command. The Tap can only be used manually and has no voice command.

As mentioned earlier, all three devices come with Bluetooth Audio Input. Only Echo Dot comes with Bluetooth Audio Output. AUX Audio Input is exclusive to the Tap, and AUX Audio Output to Echo Dot.

For Accessories, a Voice Remote can be bought separately for Amazon Echo, and is equally compatible with the Echo Dot. A 3.5mm audio cable comes standard for the Echo Dot, allowing owners to listen in on their devices. A charging cradle comes standard for the Tap, as it is built with a rechargeable, non-removable battery. The Tap also has a special sling for carry-around purposes that can be worn around.

None of these Amazon devices have Media storage.

Do I need any of these devices along with the Echo Dot?

All these products are independent with one another. Rest assured, you don't need the Echo to use the Echo Dot. There's no downside of having them both either. You simply have more devices that can also use the Alexa app, voice active or otherwise.

The Dot is a surprisingly superior device to the Echo. It may fall short on a few features, and is literally short of the taller predecessor, but they all perform the same functions. If one must choose between the Echo and Echo Dot, the Echo Dot is better and is half the price of the Echo. But if you have both, more power to your smart device music capabilities.

If you live in a small apartment building where your Echo already covers the house, then an Echo Dot is probably superfluous. But if you're in a homier accommodation, having the Dot can expand the reach of the devices hearing your wake word to them.

But the good thing about Amazon devices is that they all complement each other. As mentioned with the two Echos, they bring more sound to the house. With the Dot and Tap, you can pair the two through Bluetooth and get the best of both worlds. You speak to the Dot much like the standard Echo and get rich audio sound through the Tap. You can also carry the paired Tap around the house, listing to music and talking to Alexa just fine. The Tap and Dot are so flexible and helpful with each other that it's a boon to have both.

However, unlike most Bluetooth speakers, the Echo Dot and the media playback buttons are not compatible with one another compared to the Amazon Tap. For example, if you're listening to audio using the Echo Dot through Bluetooth speakers and for any reason want to pause or skip, you will have to ask Alexa to do it instead of manually pressing one of the buttons.

Chapter 3: Alexa Voice Service

This AI cloud service is programmed to listen to your voice and follow your commands, much like SIRI from Apple. Many of the commands you would use for the Echo Dot also work for the Echo, too (not so much the Tap, as explained last chapter). You would have to have use of this service already to be able to order the Dot, but for the sake of understanding all about your product, we'll go over Alexa's features.

Wake Word

Alexa works by voice command, and can only start or follow your commands through a wake word. For both the Echo and Echo Dot, you need to say "Alexa" before you can tell your smart device what you want. You'll know that it is ready to respond when the top blue ring spins and shines towards the direction of the person who is talking. If someone said the wake word from the west side of the room, the brightest point would be west of the Dot's ring.

But the commands are limited and the Echo Dot isn't a service robot. You can't ask it "Alexa, make me a sandwich" and expect it to grow metal limbs while searching your pantry cabinet. But you can expect the Alexa voice service to answer questions from the weather in some country of the world, or how fast a roadrunner can run.

It is, of course, possible to change the wake word to Amazon or Echo in the settings menu. In case you have someone named Alexa in your household, or are named Alexa, and want to avoid confusion of activating the smart device.

There are a number of commands to use, but the first you should remember is "Alexa, Stop". This helps keep the clutter and noise down if it is too much for you to bear.

If you have both an Amazon Echo and Amazon Echo Dot, you'll likely come to a situation where you ask Alexa to play a song (more on that later) and hear both of them activated. The Echo's are very good at listening, so the solution to limit one over the other and save electricity is to set different wake words to each device; there are three to choose from in "Alexa", "Amazon", or "Echo". Alternatively, you can separate the devices further into different rooms, especially ones with closed doors.

Music

First and foremost, Echo Dot is a smart speaker. You can ask Alexa to play whatever song you want, and after a quick search, she'll play it for you. If you want to repeat, you can say so, or if you want her to stop the music, she'll stop.

Assuming you have Amazon Prime, Alexa will stream music from Prime Music by default.

Here is a list of commands to ask Alexa during music. Again, you have to say the wake word first before following up with your request:

Play [genre]

Play [your playlist name]

Play [band name]

Play [song] by [band]

Play [station name] on [streaming device]

What's playing?

Turn it up.

Softer.

Volume (any number).

Mute.

Stop the music.

Pause.

Resume.

Next song.

Loop.

Set a sleep timer for (number) minutes.

Stop playing music in (number) minutes.

Cancel sleep timer.

Buy this song / album (*when listening through radio*).

Add this song (*while playing a song from Prime Music*).

I like this song; thumbs down (*when a song or track from Pandora / iHeartRadio / Prime Stations is playing*).

Be wary of the volume at which Alexa is playing the music. If it is too loud, the Echo Dot won't be able to hear your voice over the playback. You'll most likely have to say Alexa more than once, shout the wake word, or use the Echo Remote (accessory sold separately).

Trivia, Questions, and just plain Talking

We live in a very tech savvy age where we can access any answer to any question. The Echo Dot is a handy tool for whatever question pops into your head because it can access the internet instantly.

Your range of questions can go from broad topics to movies. Alexa will usually respond immediately for simple questions, but for those not already in her database, you will be given a list of search results (like Apple's Siri).

There are a lot of helpful questions you can ask Siri as you start the day, such as:

- Weather (will automatically tell you the weather in your Zip Code. For weather outside of that area, you need to be more specific.)

- The News (saves time waiting through a news channel, especially if you're late and/or missed one of your morning stations)

- The Time (you can also be specific in what time it is in other states or countries.)

- A Wikipedia Topic (Alexa will give you a brief summary, and then

- Pronunciation of a word ("Alexa, how to spell 'pronunciation'?")

- Science and/or Math related ("Alexa, how many cups in a gallon?" "Alexa, what is 25 times 78?" "Alexa, what is Pi?" Conversion questions are especially easy for Alexa.)

- World Trivia (Such as who won the Super Bowl of 1979, or when the Declaration of Independence was signed. These are also easy, clear answers for Alexa. However, she can't give specifics like what the winning score of the Super Bowl was)

There are many kinds of questions you can ask, and you might be surprised how much Alexa "knows".

To-Do List

On top of access to music and general knowledge, the Echo Dot can also be your personal list organizer, from daily activities to chores. Suppose you're in the kitchen and realize that you're missing out on your favorite snacks. You know you need to write a list down before you forget, but perhaps you don't have time to go shopping until later in the week. And unless you write the list down now and/or set it on a refrigerator magnet, chances are you're going to forget.

That's where Alexa can help, with the following commands:

- Alexa, add milk to my shopping list.

- Alexa, add fruit snacks to the shopping list.

- Alexa, read my shopping list.

With your handy Echo Dot, you'll have the list digitally saved and ready for the day you will go shopping, and list whatever foods you want to buy for later. Now you don't have to worry about forgetting anything except checking the list Alexa has jotted down.

You can also ask Alexa to keep tally a to-do list, like watering the garden:

- Alexa, add water the garden to my to-do list.

- Alexa, start timer for 30 minutes.

- Alexa, read my to-do list.

The timer is for tasks that don't require your full attention, whether its baking, laundry, or watering the garden. Since I use a sprinkler, I can set the water on for an extended period of time without having to use it or check up on it. The timer is also helpful, because if I accidentally leave it on too long without checking up on it, then the plants might be overwatered and ruined.

The best part is that Alexa app keeps every list stored inside, so you can reference it as you run your errands.

Multi-tasking

The biggest appeal of the voice service is that it is hands free. You can control the lights while talking on the phone, turn up the thermostat from the next hall over, add items to a shopping list while digging through a pantry, and many more options. As long as Alexa can you hear you, it's possible to ask.

As mentioned last chapter, the Amazon Echo and Echo Dot both complement each other. You can even divide the work and effort for each device. The larger Echo, for example, can be used to control the smart home appliances like the lights and thermostat, or as an alarm clock by your bed side and daily weather channel reporter. The Echo Dot can be set at the kitchen on the other side of the house, snug near the other appliances. And as you get your morning coffee and breakfast, you can ask the Dot about the news, have it turn the lights on, adjust the thermostat, act as a timer, and even entertain young children with trivia games as dinner meals are prepared.

Chapter 4: Skills

Believe it or not, your little Echo Dot can learn even more tricks, but sadly can't use them to slay monsters. Skills are like apps you can apply to the Dot that allow it more commands to follow. This includes ordering Pizza from Domino's, asking for a ride through Uber, or even opening your garage door with Garageio. This is thanks to Alexa branching out on more devices, so more third-party developers add more skills to the roaster.

That's right, more skills are being made and added all the time. And through the Alexa app, you can read the reviews and decide which ones you want to use. If you can, look up the Alexa Skills Kit (or ASK) for a collection of self-service APIs, tools, documentation and code samples that are easy and quick to apply.

The Alexa Skills Kit, in fact, is a good place to start for getting new and more skills. If you already have it, or are in the process of getting ASK, then we can bolster Alexa's horizons and capabilities. And as a bonus, these skills can work on any Amazon/Alexa device.

First off, you have to decide what you want your Alexa to do, and there two different kinds of skills you can decide from. First, you may want Alexa to have a skill that can handle any kind of request. These are called **Custom Skills.** They refer to requests including but not limited to:

- Looking up information from a web service

- integrating with a web service to order something as mentioned above (a ride from Uber, a pizza from Domino's, ect.)

- Finding and playing interactive games.

Second are **Smart Home Skills API,** or skills that let the user control cloud-enabled smart devices. These skills can allow you to:

- Turn the lights on or off.

- Change the lights to bright or dim.

- Change the temperature of a house thermostat.

It should be noted that the following steps are fairly complex, and even when there is a step-by-step process explaining what to do and what you need to know, you should only consult this chapter if you really want to know how to make skills for your Alexa and Amazon Echo Dot.

Furthermore, this chapter will assume that you already have a set up Amazon Echo Dot or an Alexa enabled-device ready. If you are still wondering how to set up Amazon Echo Dot, read on to Chapter 5 first.

The makings of a Custom Skill

By creating a custom skill, you also create:

- A series of intents and actions that allow users to freely use the skill to its core functionality.

- Sample utterances highlighting the words and phrases that can invoke the skill in question.

- An invocation name for the skill (what it's called)

- A cloud-based service to accept the intent as a request and then act on it.

- A configuration to bring all these together so Alexa can route requests to the service for the skill.

Take for example the Tide Pooler sample skill. The intent code reads as "OneshotTideIntent". There is then a list of utterances mapped out so Alexa can figure out what you're asking. The more utterances, the better; having just one utterance means you have to be that specific each time.

Say you ask: "Alexa, *get high tide for Beverly Hills* from **Tide Pooler**". The italicized words represent the uttering, while the bold represents the invocation name.

When you speak this to your Amazon Echo Dot, your speech is streamed to the cloud service, as Alexa recognizes the request it represents before sending it to the Tide Pooler service. Receiving the request and filling it into the city value (Beverly Hills), the Tide Pooler receives the request and takes the appropriate action, such as looking up the tide chart online.

After finding the information, the Pooler sends Alexa the response, to which it then responds to the user. So you might expect something like: "Today in Beverly Hills, the first high tide will be around 2:50 in the morning, and will peak at about 9 ½ feet." (Note that this is all example and not at all accurate.)

Making Conversation

A custom skill is typically what gathers information from a user's question and replies back. The use of Uber and Domino's is such an example of a custom skill because they ask Alexa to get a car from the former or a pizza from the latter. You can even ask how to make an omelet, or your daily horoscope.

Or you can bypass the question and just say "Alexa, open Tide Pooler". This is a simpler option for users that don't know the exact utterances or requests to make; even if there are a lot of utterances Alexa can accept, they have to be exactly worded or the command doesn't work. In the case of "open Tide Pooler", it allows you to start up the function easy. And should Alexa require more information, you can just make small talk.

"Alexa, get me the high tide from Tide Pooler," you say. The Amazon Echo Dot starts up the OneShotTideIntent program, but stops.

"Tide information for what city?" asks Alexa. The light ring on the Echo Dot gives a visual cue that it is ready to move on at your response.

"Beverly Hills," you reply. Alexa now makes the city search and replies promptly.

Your Skill's Visual Component

Amazon's Alexa App is not only usable on your Amazon centric devices (Echo, Echo Dot, Tap) but also the Fire OS, Android, iOS and many desktop web browsers. This makes using custom skills relevant twofold:

First, the app displays the skill detail cards for all published skills. Any user can review these cards to know what skills do what before enabling them. The more useful information provided for the skills, the more likely they can be published and used by others.

Second, the app displays home cards that can describe or enhance the user's voice interactions with Alexa. Any user can view these cards later—as to know more about what Alexa will say next—or refresh their memory of what to respond to Alexa.

You can also include content to your skill cards. For example, the Tide Pooler skill sends a home card to the user with the information they have asked for. Instead of just rallying the info, the home card can allow the user to read the information at their leisure before making another request.

Detail Card Editing

Users can scroll, search, and read through published skills listed on the Alexa app in detail cards. Before submitting the skill, you need to define the card with the relevant fields of interest for the developer portal. The better the content, the easier it is for users alike to understand and use the skill you made for everyone.

As mentioned prior, there are phrases where you can direct Alexa to do specific skills you request of, and they have to be relayed in a specific utterance order. You can create more utterances so you can have a wider range of accuracy to use the skill.

To create more phrases for your detail card, review your sample utterances and select three that you believe will help users access the skill better. Fill the valid value for any slots in those three phrases. If one of them uses a slot defined by a custom slot type, use a value that is explicitly defined for that custom slot type. For example, the {City} slot in the utterance OneshotTideIntent uses a custom slot type as "LIST_OF_CITIES". When filling this slot and asking for a high tide in a certain city like Beverly Hills, make sure it is including in the LIST_OF_CITIES.

It should go without saying at this point that you will need to use the wake word (default "Alexa") first and say it with the utterance for the invocation of your choice. For example: "Alexa, ask Tide Pooler when is high tide in Beverly Hills." Make sure the phrase is grammatically correct (Alexa will ask you to repeat if the phrasing isn't correct or clear). When you are done, enter the three phrases in the Example Phrases field on the Publishing Information tab for your skill.

Design a Voice User Interface

With a voice user interface, your skill can allow for users to interact and use it. It is the most crucial component for your skill, so you should work on this before doing any code writing.

First, create a flow diagram that maps out how users will interact with the skill. The diagram should show the requests users will make from the skill, as well as list the possible outcomes of those requests. Use this diagram when designing the detailed elements of your interface.

Next, create your *intent schema*. An intent schema is a JSON structure which declares the set of requests (aka "intents") your service can accept and handle.

And don't forget to create a set of sample utterances that can map out your intents. Remember, these will be the phrases users like yourself will use to interact with Alexa, so the clearer and easier they are, the better.

Skill Set-up

There are a few steps to creating a new skill in the developer portal and creating your service to host your code.

First, register your new skill on the developer portal. At this point, you can enter a **Name** and **Invocation Name** for your new skill.

The quickest way to start is by creating an Amazon Web Service Lambda function. The AWS Lambda is a service that lets you run code in the cloud without managing servers (and will be discussed at length with Home Skills and coding). Or you can even build a web service for your skill and host it on a cloud provider.

Writing and Testing the Skill Code

The primary coding task for your skill should be to create a service to accept requests from Alexa service, as well as send them off. If you are using Lambda, you can code in Node.js, Java, or Python (further details to Lambda are mentioned below). You are however free to use any other programming language when hosting the skill as a web service.

In the developer portal, you can fill in the rest of the information for your skill for testing. The endpoint (Lambda ARN if using Lambda), your intent schema, and sample utterances are such examples, and you should be able to test the custom skill with ease on a service simulator or Alexa-enabled device.

When the skill itself is finished, you'll need to submit it and get it certified for other Amazon customers. You do this by updating the data of the skill on the Alexa App, then testing it against the submission checklist.

This checklist has all the tests performed by Amazon's certification team. The more tests you pass, the faster the certification process goes, so complete them all if you can. Afterwards, you can submit the skill for certification.

The Ecosystem

The standard Alexa smart home ecosystem comes with the following features, and most of them will be discussed at length later in the chapter:

- The person interacting with Alexa and cloud enabled devices called "Customer"

- The "Smart Home Skill API" service, able to understand and convert voice commands into directive JSON messages.

- A computer service called "AWS Lambda" that acts as a skill adapter. Offered by Amazon Web Services, AWS LAmbda lets you run code in the cloud without managing servers. Through Alexa, you can send your code to inspect the request, take any necessary actions and then send back a response. You can write Lambda functions in Java, Node.js, or Python.Code and configure them to interpret directives and send messages to a device cloud via "smart home skill".

- The "Device Cloud", as mentioned above, allows the customer to use other cloud-enabled devices.

so you know, a customer that enables their required devices to the device cloud can say "Alexa, turn on the kitchen light" to any device, not just the Amazon Echo Dot; this means any Alexa-enabled device that hears the order and sends it to their Alexa service for interpretation. Then the Alexa Smart House Skill API interprets the action to "turn on" as the device name of "kitchen light". This is composed of a message sent to the skill adapter to control the kitchen light. This message is a directive.

The directive message is broken into three steps:

- The action (turn on)

- The device identifier (such as an ID representing the device)

- Information that shows the authenticity of the customer

Back to the skill adapter, it receives and scans the request for action, using the other details of the directive steps. This information is then sent to the device cloud via a message, telling it to turn the kitchen light on.

The device cloud, after receiving the message, does so.

And finally, the skill adapter sends a response back to the Smart Home Skill API to let you, the customer, know that the action has been carried out, and if it was successful or not. Alexa may feel the need to say "Okay" if the request has been carried out to the letter.

Developing Smart Home Skills

Anyone with the time and know-how can develop a home skill. They're easy to make thanks to Amazon's voice interactions. The Alexa service knows how to interpret the user's speech and what messages you can send to your smart home skills. These smart home skills can be developed in two different ways:

There are the developers that represent cloud-connected device manufacturers that want to enable customers to interact with the devices using your voice. And there are the developers that want to create an Alexa skill for cloud-connected devices for private or public use (there needs to be certification for the latter).

Prerequisites to Smart Home Skill Development

One can't just start making skills for their Amazon device. You need to have each of the following:

- An Amazon developer account, which is free to sign up for.

- A connected device with a cloud API.

- An Alexa-enabled device (Amazon Echo, Amazon Echo Dot, Amazon Tap)

- An AWS account. You can host your skill adapter as an AWS Lambda function and double up that way.

- Some knowledge of programming languages such as Java, Node.js and Python. Lambda functions can be written into those same languages.

- Basic understanding of how OAuth 2.0 works (OAuth is short for Open Authorization). It allows a resource owner like yourself use and access resource providers (such as Facebook) through a third party social network.

First, you create a smart home skill in the Amazon developer portal. You provide this new skill with information, configuration, and an endpoint: the skill adapter. The Skill Adapter is an AWS Lambda function that handles requests from the Smart Home Skill API and talks through the device cloud. This communication should be enabled through the device cloud and an OAuth 2.0 authorization grant code. You'll need this information about the authentication endpoint, client ID, and secret to complete the smart home skill registration.

Create a Skill as a Developer

To make a free developer account, you need to make one on the Amazon Developer Portal. The website you can go to is https://developer.amazon.com/login.html. Once registered, open the Amazon Developer Portal in a browser and log in. Navigate to the Alexa section via the Apps & Services tap. Click that, and then click Alexa at the top navigation.

In the Alexa Skills Kit box, go to Get Started, and then Add a New Skill button. Through the Skill Information page, select Smart Home Skill API and enter the designated Name for your Skill. Save the skill, then copy the application ID for it to the clipboard.

Create a Lambda Function

Again, you need a AWS account, as well as some knowledge about AWS. The skill adapter portion of your smart home skill is hosted ala Lambda function on AWS, which allows you to run code in the device cloud without managing servers.

With your AWS Account, you can create your Lambda function. To get started, go on the AWS Console, look under Compute, and select Lambda. Look for the region tab in the upper right corner, and select N. Virginia. This is important because North Virginia is currently the only region with Lambda function support. Now click Create a Lambda function.

There are three following steps. Step 1 is select a blueprint page. For the purpose of example, type "home" in the filter box, and select the "alexa-smart-home-skill-adapter".

Step 2 is to configure the event sources page, which should be configured to Alexa Smart Home. You can also add the Application Id from the developer portal.

And Step 3 is the Configure function. Enter the **Name** of the Lambda function, the **Description** of it, and the **Runtime** (either Python, Node.js or Java). And remember to have the edit code inline selected for the Lambda function code.

Copy and paste that very code into the code editor. It'll provide a starting point for implementing a skill adapter, as well as determining the request type via the namespace and name values in the message header. The namespaces may determine whether the request is made a discovery or a control request. They'll be called "handleDiscovery" or "handleControl" functions respectively.

For a control request, the name property specifies the kind of request. For instance, the only request type on this example code we're making is a "TurnOnRequest". The response isn't fully implemented yet, though you should handle every type of request a user would make to your skill, as well as give the right response headers and pay off.

For the Handler space, leave the default name:

"lambda_function.lambda_handler". It's simpler that way, as that handler is the entry point for a lambda function. You can specify it with the format "filemName.entryPointFunctionName." When you edit code inline in the console, the file name is "lambda_function" and the "lambda_handler" function acts as the entry point. Make sure your role selection is "Lambda_basic_execution" role.

For Role, select Lambda_basic_execution role. Unless you REALLY know what you're doing, leave the advanced settings as is and move on.

Now we're on Step 4: the review page. Take the time to look it over and make sure everything is to your satisfaction. Ignore the Enable event source button; you can do it after the function implication is complete. Now create the function.

On the summary page, copy the Amazon Resource Name, or ARN, for the Lambda function. This will be found in the upper right corner in your clipboard, and you will use the value given to configure your smart home skill.

Now you'll need to finish registering your skill via configuration by OAuth 2.0. After logging in, navigate back to the Developer Portal via Alexa section under Apps and Services. Your skill should be on the displayed list, so click it.

Skip the Interaction model tap, as it is already predefined. When you get to the Configuration page, copy the ARN number in the Endpoint field from your Lambda function. Enable Account Linking for your skill, so end-users can associate their cloud-enabled devices with the Alexa skill. Basically that means you need to connect an Alexa user with an account in your system, and provide an access token that uniquely identifies the user within your system. Through the token, your skill can now be used to authenticate the system on behalf of the user.

Be sure to note that a OAuth provider must have a certificate signed by someone with authority by Amazon or else the link will fail. You will also need the following fields for certification required:

- Authorization ULR (the login page to your website)

- Client ID (your identifier used to recognize the request coming from your skill. You will use the authorization code grant)

- Redirect URL (Your URL which you are sent to after successfully logging in. Enabling account linking displays this as well)

- Authorization Grant Type (preselected, and supported by Smart Home Skill API)

You need to fill out the following for the Authorization Grant Type:

- Client Secret (a credential allowing you to use Alexa service and their Access Tokens)

- Client Authentication Scheme (Identifies the type of authentication via requesting tokens)

- Privacy Policy URL (a page where you talk about private policy. Required for Smart Home Skills)

Finally, enable testing (via Yes) on the Test Page.

The Test Run

When your implementation is complete, and the skill adapter in Lambda has worked well, you can now test how well and functional your new smart home skill runs on your Amazon Echo Dot. First, make sure the event source is enabled. Then select your smart home skill via Lambda console, and Alexa Smart Home through the Event sources tab.

If the state is already enabled, skip it. But if the state is disabled, click it and re-enable it again.

Find your skill in the Alexa app, enable and account-link your skill to the device cloud it is designed to work with. Go to Skills and search the name of your smart home skill if you're having trouble finding it. If you want to remove account linking later, you can disable your skill in the skills tab. Manage your devices in the Your Devices section of Smart Home. After testing the skill with valid and invalid voice commands, you can send in the new home skill to be certified. This is the final step.

Certification

Another procedure: go back to the development portal, and this time look for "Get Started" under the Alexa section tab. Select your smart home skill and head for the Publishing Information page. You should see your skill here with the following items to be filled: Descriptions, Category, Keywords, Images, Test Instructions. Category is fixed on Smart Home.

Afterwards, you'll get a privacy and compliance page, then you'll answer some questions and be able to submit your home skill for certification. Now you just sit back and wait, with a few earned pats on the back for a job (hopefully) well done.

Chapter 5: How to Set up your Amazon Echo Dot

Because of how similar in hardware the Echo Dot is to its predecessor, the set-up process will be the same as well. You should be fine if you remember how to set up your Echo, but if you don't remember or have never bought an Echo prior to the Echo Dot, then this chapter will help guide you through the process.

Unboxing

Firstly, you'll need to have ordered the Amazon Echo Dot. You can only do so through the Alexa voice service, which you can buy from the App Store on your iOS or Android. She doubles as a helpful (if not a tad obnoxious) verbal guide through the step by step process, so you can either trust in her or read on. Or do both, and refer to this book as a handy reference step by step.

Charge it up

Anyway, with the app ready, you can unpack your Echo Dot and plug it in to your outlet.

You'll know it's on a̶n̶ ̶ ̶ ̶ ̶ing when the indicator ring flashes blue, and then orange. This means it can be configured with your home Wi-Fi information. If you don't set it up right away and Alexa starts complaining (and/or the ring turns purple), hold down the action button (the button opposite the mute button) for five seconds until it turns orange again. Alexa might be set too loudly, so take this time to adjust the volume by turning the top disc.

Configure

Once the Echo Dot is fully charged and still in orange-configuration-mode, pull out your Smartphone and open up the Wi-Fi settings. Like many smart-home products, the Echo Dot requires you to ad-hoc connect directly to it during the configuration process in order to input configuration info.

Select the Echo Dot's Wi-Fi connection; you'll have to look for the one that reads Amazon in the name. After that is set up, then you should be able to launch the Amazon Alexa App to begin the configuration. In case the app doesn't go right into configuration, tap the menu icon, specifically over the three-internet status bars in the upper left corner, and select Settings.

"Your Echo Dot"

Through the Settings menu, you can select one of two things. If you personally purchased the Echo on your Amazon account, then there should be an Echo Dot with your name next to it: "[Your Name]'s Echo Dot". All Alexa devices are named after the one who purchased it, and have their voices recognized by them. But in the off chance you were given the Echo Dot as a gift, won it as a prize, or simply did not purchase it yourself, you can select "Set up new device" to fix that.

By now you are connected to the Echo's ad-hoc network and with the app up and running, the rest is easy. Now you can input your Amazon account login credentials, agree to the Alexa user conditions (as in, you're OK with your voice being sent to Amazon to be analyzed for commands and service improvements), and finally select your Wi-Fi network from the list of networks available from the Echo Dot's list.

Chapter 6: Bluetooth

A Primer

Bluetooth is a new popular wireless technology innovation that allows two devices to "talk" to each other. This can be seen in a number of ways, such as a speakerphone device that allows you to connect your phone to it so you can talk hands free while driving.

In the case of Bluetooth speakers, your smartphone, tablet, or any other device transmits to the Bluetooth speaker, where it usually has a build-in amplifier and stronger sound than the smaller device. This allows for better and crisper sound quality than originally. For example, the speakerphone mentioned prior to be heard loud enough for everyone in the car to talk back to the person on the other end.

Connecting/pairing your device to a Bluetooth speaker is a simple onetime operation. Most Bluetooth speakers will remember and recognize your phone when in range, so after your initial pairing, all you have to do is turn the speaker on. After that, you are ready to listen and play. There is one thing you need to remember though: even though Bluetooth speakers are wireless, they still need power for their built-in amplifier. Some speakers will always need to be plugged into a wall outlet to work. A model with a rechargeable battery is recommended for those that look for portability.

Echo Dot Speakers

Because the Echo Dot is a proportionally smaller product to the original Echo, there had to be changes. It manages to keep all the core features, and comes with stereo sound, but the size still impairs its ability to carry sound. If placed side by side, a smartphone would sound louder and clearer.

On the plus side, the Echo Dot's Bluetooth speakers are some of the best of a product that small, and not many other Bluetooth speakers come with a wide variety of features either.

Also, because it is a Bluetooth speaker, you have the ability to listen to sounds and songs through speakers much larger than the Echo.

The Echo cannot pair itself to Bluetooth speakers. It can sense and pair up with

Bluetooth-enabled devices like smartphones, but that's it. But that's fine, as it provides a rich quality of sound in its small package.

Yes, you can easily pair any Bluetooth speaker to the Echo Dot—pairing it with a quality speaker like the Nyne Bass means instant wireless and rich sound. But that's just the beginning. As mentioned in the Differences chapter, the Echo Dot works with both Bluetooth Outputs *and* Inputs; it doesn't discriminate. In other words, you can link a nice pair of Bluetooth headphones to it just as easily as speakers.

It helps is that there's a 3.5 stereo jack on the back of the Echo Dot, and that you come with the same size cable in your order. You can not only plug headphones into your Echo Dot, but plug your Echo Dot into any home stereo system for better sound quality. The regular Echo is seriously lacking in compatibility.

There's a catch however: if your stereo is set to a different input—like your TV instead of your Echo Dot—you won't hear any audio from the Echo Dot. Even Alexa will be muted out. The sound goes all to stereo, which doesn't make much sense for how the Dot was made and supposed to be used. Sadly, TV configuration, let alone specific stereo configuration is different for each brand. It would take too much time to go over each and every brand, as well as deviate away from the main purpose of this book. If you wish to set your Echo Dot to your stereo system, I suggest asking professional help or looking it up online. Otherwise, you are on your own.

Chapter 7: A Bedtime companion

With all these features in mind, what's the best place to put your small but functional smart speaker? There are many places from the main room to the kitchen where you can relax and listen to music. The bottom of the Echo Dot has a very sticky, rubbery surface too, that acts kind of like glue. Thanks to this, the whole device does not move when you turn the volume knob on the top. The device is relatively light compared to the full sized Amazon Echo, so it needs something to act as the anchor.

This makes it ideal to place the Dot anywhere in the room and not worry about it being knocked over or moved. The surface is so sticky it can even stay firmly planted on a window (though that's a pretty dangerous place to put a Dot so don't consider it).

With its acute sound speakers and sticky bottom, any room would be ideal. But I believe the best place for the Echo Dot is in your room. Even more so than the Echo. After all, Echo is more for big rooms and can carry sound further out, like in the kitchen or living room. The Echo Dot is a bit softer, much smaller, and looks almost like a coaster. What better place for such a device than on your nightstand?

Audible

Audible is Amazon's online book store, which you can purchase and read on your mobile devices like Kindle. All of the books found here can be found and bought at very manageable prices for as low as $0.99. You can even find eBooks like the one you're reading now on Amazon's online store.

So how does this help? Alexa can not only play music, but she can read you stories when given the proper command. Whether it's the next chapter of A Song of Fire and Ice series, or a bedtime story for your little ones, you can just say "Alexa, Read Game of Thrones", or "Alexa, Read Goodnight Moon". In case Alexa has some trouble findig the books, specify "-from Audible".

To further enhance the bedtime story reading experience, throw in the command "Alexa, set a sleep timer for X minutes".

Meditation/Exercise

Perhaps you like to think of yourself as a physically active person? Another idea to ease yourself to sleep is through meditation, or the practice of calming your mind.

Assuming you're already an Amazon Prime subscriber, you'll find tons of meditations you can add right to your library. They're perfect not for morning or afternoon routines, but you can at least one sleep meditation video. It's called "Guided Meditation for Restful Sleep" and even if you're not a subscriber, it's only 99 cents to buy so it's easily affordable.

Once you've added your ideal meditation "music" to your library, you can ask Alexa to play the audio.

This also works for work out routines, from playing work out music to other meditation choices. If you like to start every morning with a quick set of push-ups and/or sit-ups, Alexa can be your handy trainer.

White Nose

Some people find white noise to help them fall asleep. Like the meditations mentioned earlier, you can find "sleeping sounds" that are free to add to your library as part of your Prime subscription, or buy them at just below a dollar.

It might take some experimentation for Alexa to know which track to play, or what white sound works best for you. Try remembering the entire track name, or else she will be confused and play a different track from a different album. Say you bought and want to hear the first track from "Thunderstorms & Rain". You'll need to say, "Alexa, play Soothing Rain Effects and Distant Thunder Showers" or else she may not recognize what you want.

Alarm Clock

Music, exercise, story reading, questions, trivia... and an alarm clock too? There's truly no shortage of what the Echo Dot (or the Echo for that matter) can do. If you need to wake up early tomorrow, you can set the command "Alexa, set an alarm for 6 AM". If you have a regular job the requires you to wake up that early every day, you can slip in the word "repeating" before "alarm". E.g. "Alexa, set a repeating alarm for 6 AM".

The default alarm is pleasant enough to wake up to, but Amazon gives you a wide range of choices to choose from. You can even set your alarm to some celebrities like Alec Baldwin.

To peruse and choose a new sound, open the Alexa app, tap Menu, then Timers & Alarms. Tap on Alarms, then Manage alarm volume and default sound. Tap Alarm Default Sound and you'll look through a whole list of options to choose from. For that old-school styled alarm clock ring, go for Nightstand.

Other Wake Up Options.

In case you don't want to wake up to an alarm, there are other suggestions you can give to Alexa. Like your old radio cassette player, you can have Alexa play music from your favorite radio station. But how can you do what when you're asleep?

A loophole you can try is record yourself saying "Alexa, play Kiss 1.08", and set it as your alarm sound for the alarm app on your smartphone. Your phone wakes up first to your designated hour, and tells Alexa for you to play your favorite music.

It sounds kind of convoluted, yes, and you can probably just set a music alarm to your smartphone to save time, but wouldn't you like to rely more on your Alexa?

Speaking of, Android users should check out Alarm Clock 3, which supports custom audio files. If you're an iPhone owner, you can use the built-in Clock app and choose your custom sound from the Add Alarm menu. Just remember to record the sound first with a voice recorder beforehand.

Waking up to the Light

Finally, studies have shown that it's much better to wake up to gradual light than to a blaring alarm. The Echo Dot works with a variety of smart-home lighting systems and switches, from the Belkin Insight Switch to Philips Hue. Not to mention Bluetooth connections.

But here's something really interesting. You can pair up your Echo Dot to something like a Lifx lightbulb. You're probably surprised how that works, especially when Lifx is not displayed under the Connected Home menu in Settings through the Alexa App.

You can still get it to work by installing the Lifx app to your phone and have at least one Lifx bulb added to your Lifx Cloud account. Then you open the Lifx app on your phone and scroll to the bottom. Look for the Integrations section, tap the Amazon Echo Dot button, and login to your Amazon account. Tap Authorize to give your Echo Dot access to the Lifx bulbs.

Now you can open the Amazon Alexa app, head to the Settings page and select Connected Home. Scroll to the bottom and tap "Discover Devices". This app will scan for wireless networks, and yours should allow Lifx to be connected and accessible to your Amazon Echo Dot (or any Amazon smart device you want to set it up to, like the Echo).

In order to control the bulbs better, you will need to create new groups for your Lifx bulbs. These will not the same groups created within the Lifx app, but you are free to use the same names for the groups. For simplicity's sake, have the group names be the same as the rooms as the bulbs are in. Living Room, Office, Bedroom, etcetera.

Now that you have the Lifx bulbs linked and connected, you can use commands like "Alexa, turn office lights on." That being said, your control over the Lifx bulbs is very limited without activating the Lifx skill. To enable this, go to the Skills section within the Alexa app. Search for Lifx and tap **Enable**. In the window that opens, login to your Lifx Cloud account and authorize the connection.

With this enabled, you are given better control over the lights. You can now say things like "Alexa, tell Lifx to change office lights to full brightness," or "Alexa, tell Lifx to make living room lights blue."

You could also set up various recipes with IFTTT to control the Lifx lights, as well as a host of devices around your house with very specific voice commands. In other words, you can experiment with Alexa and IFTTT to make different voice commands.

For example, you have a Lifx that actives with the video lights. Following "Alexa, trigger video lights", the lamp in the back of the video room will change brightness, and possibly color too. You can have the color change be specific through Alexa, such as "Alexa, tell Lifx to turn my office lights blue." You can also set the brightness, like "Alexa, tell Lifx to set the brightness to 40%." These phrases might be a bit verbose and hard to get through, but they have a high response and success time.

With IFTTT integration, even a single phrase can trigger multiple recipes. Telling "Alexa, (to) trigger video lights" could also be programmed to turn the AC off with Nest, or toggle the rest of the lights in the apartment off, or turn off any other particularly noisy appliances that are plugged into smart switches. Using a single Echo and/or Echo Dot command like this is very handy.

Finally, and the main appeal to triggering lights with your bed buddy Echo Dot, you can set your app via IFTTT to "slowly turn on Lifx lights when an Amazon Echo (Dot) alarm goes off".

Conclusion

Thank you again for downloading this book!

I hope this book was able to help you to learn all about your Amazon Echo Dot and know how to use it like a pro.

The next step is to explore the Amazon store for more features. Buy more skills for Alexa to learn, buy more books to read on audible, and buy more music to listen to whenever you fancy. The Echo Dot and Alexa are only limited by what information and data they have at hand, so the more you give her, the better.

Finally, if you enjoyed this book, please take the time to share your thoughts and post a review on Amazon. It'd be greatly appreciated!

Thank you and good luck!

References

Amazon Echo Dot Review: An Inch and a half of Alexa may be all you need – http://www.androidcentral.com/amazon-echo-dot-review

What's the Difference Between the Amazon Echo and Echo Dot? – http://www.howtogeek.com/248590/whats-the-difference-between-the-amazon-echo-and-echo-dot/

Turn your Amazon Echo Dot into the ultimate nightstand accessory – http://www.cnet.com/how-to/turn-your-amazon-echo-dot-into-the-ultimate-nightstand-accessory/

One year after Alexa: Amazon's Echo has found a small but smart niche – http://arstechnica.com/gadgets/2016/05/one-year-after-alexa-amazons-echo-has-found-a-small-but-smart-niche/

Echo Dot review: Hands-on with Amazon's smart, squat, almost-too-independent Alexa

sibling –
http://www.geekwire.com/2016/echo-dot-amazons-squat-almost-independent-alexa-sibling/

Amazon.com: Echo Dot –
http://www.amazon.com/Amazon-Echo-Dot-Portable-Bluetooth-WiFi-Speaker-with-Alexa/b?ie=UTF8&node=14047587011

Differences Between Echo, Echo Dot, and Amazon Tap –
https://www.amazon.com/gp/help/customer/display.html?nodeId=202009700

Alexa and Alexa Device FAQ –
https://www.amazon.com/gp/help/customer/display.html?nodeId=201602230

Amazon Echo Dot Review –
http://www.cnct.com/products/amazon_echo_dot-review/

Amazon Tap Review –
http://www.cnet.com/products/amazon-tap-review/

How to Set Up and Configure Your Amazon Echo – http://www.howtogeek.com/235653/how-to-set-up-and-configure-your-amazon-echo/?tag=823814-20

Video: How Bluetooth® Speakers Work – http://www.crutchfield.com/S-KeohhdgrLsh/learn/video-how-blueooth-speakers-work.html

How to connect Lifx bulbs to the Amazon Echo – http://www.cnet.com/how-to/how-to-connect-lifx-bulbs-to-the-amazon-echo/

10 Things to know about the Amazon Echo Dot – http://www.aftvnews.com/10-things-to-know-about-the-amazon-echo-dot/

Getting Started with the Alexa Skills Kit - https://developer.amazon.com/public/solutions/alexa/alexa-skills-kit/getting-started-guide

Understanding the Different Types of Skills - https://developer.amazon.com/public/solutions/alexa/alexa-skills-kit/docs/understanding-the-different-types-of-skills

Steps to Build a Custom Skills - https://developer.amazon.com/public/solutions/alexa/alexa-skills-kit/overviews/steps-to-build-a-custom-skill

Submitting an Alexa Skill for Certification - https://developer.amazon.com/public/solutions/alexa/alexa-skills-kit/docs/publishing-an-alexa-skill

Understanding the Smart Home Skill API - https://developer.amazon.com/public/solutions/alexa/alexa-skills-kit/overviews/understanding-the-smart-home-skill-api

Steps to Create a Smart Home Skill - https://developer.amazon.com/public/solutions/alexa/alexa-skills-kit/docs/steps-to-create-a-smart-home-skill

Amazon Echo Dot review: here comes the Alexa army - http://www.theverge.com/2016/4/5/11364786/amazon-echo-dot-review-alexa

Made in the USA
San Bernardino, CA
13 July 2016